super guppy

Poems by Edward van de Vendel

TRANSLATED BY DAVID COLMER

WITH ILLUSTRATIONS BY
FLEUR VAN DER WEEL

THE EMMA PRESS

THE EMMA PRESS

First published in the UK in 2019 by The Emma Press
Originally published in Dutch in 2003 as *Superguppie* in
Amsterdam, by Em. Querido's Uitgeverij.

This publication has been made possible with financial support
from the Dutch Foundation for Literature.

Text © Edward van de Vendel 2003
Illustrations © Fleur van de Weel 2003
Translation © David Colmer 2019

A CIP catalogue record of this book is available
from the British Library

Printed in Latvia by Jelgavas tipogrāfija on Arctic Volume White

ISBN 978-1-910139-65-3

The Emma Press Ltd
Registered in England and Wales, no. 08587072
Website: theemmapress.com
Email: hello@theemmapress.com
Jewellery Quarter, Birmingham, UK

N ederlands
N letterenfonds
dutch foundation
for literature

Supported using public funding by
ARTS COUNCIL
ENGLAND

Super Guppy

OTHER TITLES FROM THE EMMA PRESS

contents

beach

The sun's made all the grown-ups droop –
they've wilted like limp lettuce.
Six mothers on a bed of sand,
I think they need a helping hand.
Hey!
We told you not to wet us!

glasses

My glasses fell. They broke their arm.
They need help. They've come to harm.
But I can't see. My eyes are red.
What happens now? They're almost dead.

washing up

I want wheels,
I want wheels,
and an engine in our house.
Wheels on the kitchen,
so we can all go out.
Then Mum can have a drive
and Dad might make us crash,
and when we do the washing up,
the water will just splash.
And if I let a good plate slip –
clang, crack, smash.
Look what you've done! – I'll say, Sorry,
I'm not so good with dishes.
This road we're on is lots of fun,
but the bends are vicious.

party

What did I get when I turned two?
Books, blocks and a ball.
And what did I get at three?
Cars, cars, cars (and that was all).
But what about when I was one?
I... got... something...
I suppose.
But what exactly, no one knows.
So three cheers for me, hip-hip-hooray:
I'm having a party,
we're starting right away!
You bring presents and we'll have fun –
it's my catch-up birthday,
for turning one.

fish

Little fishy wants to speak up,
little fishy looks at me.
She opens her mouth to shout,
but I don't have a clue
what fishy's on about.
But what am I supposed to do?
I'm deaf to water-talking,
and fish are cute
but people-speaking mute.

puddle

Whassat?
Whose two mucky feet
are planted in a puddle?
Whassat?
Who's started jumping up
so that the mud'll splatter
on his socks and shorts and shirt
as if a bit of dirt
just doesn't matter.

Whassat? says my father,
looking at my clothes.
Whassat? says my father,
holding his nose.
Dad, I say,
it wasn't me,
it was the puddle.
It loved me so much,
it gave me a cuddle.

cat

Do cats make plans?
When my cat's lying on my tummy,
does she think,
Mmm, a mouse would be yummy.
I'll kill one a bit later?
Does the idea make her purr?
And does she think I'm patting her
because I like it too?
I bend down to her ear
and whisper, Tonight,
the mice will all be chasing you.

telephone

When you call
you get connected
by a line right through the air.
Someone else rings up later,
people phoning everywhere.
Hello, hello, is that you?
Six times to and fro,
threads that grow and grow,
branching more and more
until, before you know it,
you're the middle of a web
stretching over the sky.
If you pick up
you're a spider –
if you hang up
you're a fly.

chickens

Where's the volume
on the cockerel?
Where's the off switch
on the chickens?
They walk funny,
with little hiccups,
like slow robots,
wind-up clowns.
All that crowing
in the morning.
Daddy yawning –
Turn 'em down.

snow

A snowflake blobs
into my ear.
Hey! Snow!
This is me here!
What do you take me for?
Some kind of slot machine,
to win or lose?
Just put in a coin and see what I do –
run back inside
where it's nice and warm
or stay out and start a snowball fight?
Alright, winter,
you win.
Now chuck a few more snowflakes in.

plaster

The plaster on my knee's
in trouble.
Not for doing something wrong –
but for being there too long!
It's got to go.
But does it know?
If it did would it say,
Please,
just one more day.
No way this scab
is hard enough.
Ow, not so rough!
That makes Mum just pull it faster.
Goodbye, plaster.

storm

The weather blows into my room.
Windows open – whoosh and zoom,
the curtains flap me out of bed,
and with my sleepy head
I look around.
The wind dies down.
I whisper, Hello, storm,
did you get tired too?
I breathe and breathe
and breathe
like you.

guppy

I turned my back
and just like that,
all my guppies were swimming
inside the cat –
well, I guess they're not swimming anymore.
She fished them out of the bowl
with her paw.
And only left me one.
Did she leave him till last
and then forget?
Or was he too fast?
Maybe.
I don't care.
He's my lucky guppy.
He doesn't give up, he's… Super Guppy!
He stuck it out –
and that's what counts.

blackbird

I saw a blackbird
folded up dead
at the station.
And I couldn't get it into my head.
How people came and went
and no one stopped and bent
to cover it up.
They stepped over it instead.
I couldn't get it into my brain.
How Mum just started running
and said, *Hurry up,*
we'll miss our train.

16

cooker

Mum's standing at the stove.
She fiddles with the dials.
Gas whispers, *hisssssssss*
and then goes PLOF!
or
FLOOP!
or
FLOP –
or whatever it is.
What do you call that sound?
Maybe I should ask around
if anybody knows.
What's the word
when whispering explodes?

fun

On the beach
the old folks stand
and stare at silver balls
spread on the sand.
My grandad's there.
He points and waves at me.
Does that mean he won?
They're playing old-folks' games
and having old-folks' fun.
The sun is shining at last
and everything is going super slow.
Slow?
No. Old-folks' fast.

piano

Mum's playing the piano.
She puts her fingers in its mouth,
pressing down
on big white teeth.
They ring true to me.
But when she pounds
the rotten black ones.
Ow!
Toothache sounds.

shoes

My two shoes
have got big hungry mouths.
They need food
and I know what
they want to eat.
My feet.

Are they thirsty too?
Do they need something wet?
I'd better run up a sweat.

foam

Grown-up men all have to shave.
That's the way
they start their day.
Fingers full of frothy white
till their lips are out of sight.
In the mirror at their place,
every morning,
cake-fight face.

wardrobe

Dad's wardrobe
is my cubbyhole –
I burrow in there
like a mole
and live between his shirts
and coats and scarves.
So when he gets out of the bath
and needs some clothes,
he has to knock
and hope I'm home
and ask for jeans, a vest or socks.
Knock-knock.
Who's there?
It's Dad. – Dad who? –
Dad in need of underwear.

garden

We're giving the garden a makeover,
a summer takeover:
combing the grass,
trimming the hedges,
weeding the path,
doing the edges.
Lipstick colours everywhere,
flower perfume in the air.
With a summer smile on its face,
our garden is a different place.

father christmas

Christmas is a lot of fun,
but it's always gone so fast –
can't we do it in reverse
to make the season last?
Let Father Christmas stay all year
and if he needs time off,
if he really needs to get away,
he can leave
on Christmas Eve
and come back Boxing Day.

hair

Where do all the loose hairs go?
Grandad hasn't got any –
it's not fair.
So Mum, if you've got some spare,
let them fly out of your comb
all the way to Grandad's home.
Is the wind going to blow
that way today?
What's the forecast say?
Sorry, Grandad, no!

26

stepladder

Mum's got out the ladder,
the kitchen steps.
Is it House Olympics time again?
Are the games about to start?
We're cheering from the floor.
The next events are
dusting shelves and washing windows –
Mummy, you can win those!
And maybe even more!
Win them for the team!

Why doesn't she climb on up?
What's that look supposed to mean?

sugar

A pack of sugar split and leaked
in the supermarket.
Now – this makes me smile –
there's a long thin strip of beach
running down the aisle.

Nothing much to do there:
no deckchairs,
sea
or sun.
Life there's sweet,
but soon someone will come
to hoover up
the summer fun.

mitten

A mitten had gone missing
and lay there on the sand,
but what I saw
was a cut-off hand.
Not what I'd planned.
There was no blood in sight,
so I hadn't looked right.
Who should I trust,
my head or my eyes?
Who tells the most lies
when there's something to prove?
Should I have waited
for the mitten to move?

letter

I write a message in the sand
with the toes of my foot,
with the fingers of my hand.
The waves roll in to read it
and take it out to sea
and to the other shore,
which never answers me.
Or does it?
Are the waves its way of saying,
Here, let me wipe that page clean
so you can write some more.

coats

Today's a day off for our coats.
Today's the day we let them float
up in the air
above the square
like big fat butterflies.

To our surprise
they fall straight down
and lie there in a big sad pile.
We watch them for a while.
They're much too heavy things,
these winter wings.

bells

The church bells sound frightened,
they call loud and long
that something has happened,
and gone badly wrong,
that somebody's lost
or somebody's late,
that –
no, wait.
They've stopped.
They're quiet again.
As if to say,
Sorry –
got carried away!

sleep

I'm in bed
but I can't sleep,
because downstairs there's a party
and it's crashing through my head.
Grown-ups having fun
and I'm not there,
and they don't care
that I can hear it all.

I wish they'd go away.
I feel as sad and small
and lonely
as a soggy canapé.

heart

With him out there on the street,
I knew for sure:
my snowman has a heart that beats.
I felt it.
But last night the snow all melted.
My snowman disappeared.
The winter flew the coop
without a word.
And the heart?
That flew off too.
As an icy bird.

spit

Some kid keeps spitting on the ground.
They do it here,
they do it there,
they do it everywhere.
Why do they need to leave a trail?
Wet and shining like a snail's?
Are they lost?
Is that it?
Leaving a track
to find their way back
with breadcrumbs made of spit?

hands

We're walking down a busy street
past men who don't have teeth.
Past hands they're holding out.
Homeless,
says my mum.
She takes me by the hand
and hurries on.
No.
No.
No one looks at them.
No one stops to chat.
No friendly people in this town,
just people who walk fast
and don't look back.
I don't mean it to be funny,
but think as I run past:
I'm glad I'm small enough
to still get pocket money.

bed

Mum tucks me in at night
and sends me off to sleep
in a duvet envelope.
Night post,
she says,
then presses her soft lips
on mine.
And that's the stamps, she says,
*the extra stamps, to guarantee
they send you back to me
tomorrow morning.*
And then I'm yawning.
And then she says,
Sleep tight,
little letter,
Goodnight.

bang

I wanted to prove
in my room
that I knew how
to build stuff –
all by myself –
with a hammer,
and *ow*,
it went wrong,
my finger started turning blue.
But Mum knew what to do.
She came running,
gently rubbing my sore finger.
Whispering, 'Poor thing...'
and loving all the pain away.
Oh,
I could hammer every day.

outside

Miss,
you keep staring
out the window
at thin air.
But we're here, not there.
Are you looking for birds?
Do you miss the way they sing?
Do you wish that you had wings?
Miss –
this classroom's our cage
and we're stuck here all day.
Can you teach us how to fly away?

morning

I'm lying here
waiting for later.
My breaths are soft,
like little waves,
with both my eyes
closed tight,
like seashells
shutting out
the day.
Maybe the morning
is a beach
with the sun about to rise.
That must be why
there's sand in my eyes.

wet

I'm on the edge
of the swimming pool.
Not splashing,
sitting still,
and thinking carefully
about what I'd rather be:
a frog
or a boy
like me.
What's the difference?

The jump?
The joy?

car

Dad's covered in blood and looks a real sight.
Black blood from the car, it's not working right.

It needs a new carb, that's like a car heart.
A big operation. It won't even start.

Dads are like doctors who keep cars alive,
and when they're all better they go for a drive.

eyebrows

Sometimes I have a good close look
at Grandad's bushy eyebrows.
They're big and beautiful,
like grass or straw
that's had years
and years to dry
above his eyes:
a little farm
for tiny sweat animals.
Look, there's some!
It's hot, and here they come:
droplet piglets
slowly
making their way
down his forehead
to shelter in the hay.

park

Seven men with rakes
giving a patch
of park
a gentle scratch.

A bouncy dog,
all jumpy and titchy,
thinks,
That's fun! The grass is itchy!
He wants to help and races round,
throwing up big clumps of ground.

Seven men
by the flowerbeds
scratch their chins
and shake their heads.

newspaper

Who brings the papers every day
while we're all sound asleep?
Each door,
a hungry mouth.
The letterboxes,
snapping jaws.
Breakfast delivery
on our street
and news is what
we want to eat.

chair

It can take forever –
an introduction to a chair.
I mean: Hello, there!
I'm Boris. Boris. Boris.
Boris.
Yes.
Being introduced to a chair
takes ten minutes or maybe more.
I mean – four legs to shake
hands with. Four.
Four.
4.

summer

First I burn
and then I peel
in little flakes and strips.
I pick them off
and fit them in
a picture of myself.
Summer's a puzzle –
you solve it with your skin.

50

window

Hello, birdy,
silly birdy,
flapping at the glass.
Why don't you just fly on past?
There's nothing for you here inside.
No midges, gnats or flies.
Don't get me wrong.
I like your song,
but you don't need to come this close.
What can I say?
'Birdy, silly birdy,
why don't you fly
away?'

fruit

Shall we play fruit bowls?
You're a peach,
and I'm an apricot.
Here we go, ready or not.
First we'll reach out
and stroke each other's skin.
If that's alright,
we'll take a bite.
Don't tell anyone.
Sweet and tasty,
nice and round.
Afterwards we'll put each other back –
upside-down.

shadow

We form a circle
and look down –
and see us lying there.
Six flat friends all in a ring,
six shadows on the ground.
Six flat friends
with eyes shut tight
all painted on the floor
with paint that's made
of darkened light –
and now we'll play some more.

ice

Winter's turned the pond
into a table
of ice.
I walk out on it
and go sliding –
once, twice,
a dozen times.
Watery fun without getting wet –
what are we playing?
Frozen serviette.

wrinkles

Grandma's face is crumpled –
with lines where her smiles got stuck.
Steal one for good luck,
she says, pointing to her cheek.
I say,
Grandma, you're sweet.
And then she gets even more lines
so I grab them too.
She laughs,
You little wrinkle thief, you!

shower

Whoosh!
The water from the shower
powers down –
and right away I'm fully dressed
in a skin-tight water-suit
with water-pants, a water-vest,
water-cap and water-boots,
water-gloves and a water-top.
Oh – why's it have to stop?
Water clothes all washed away.
Water coolness here to stay.

dream

I dreamt I was dreaming
and then I woke up.
But I was still dreaming,
so *then* I woke up.
It was like tumbling –
jumping up
and then stumbling,
over and over and over again –
or was that a dream too?
It's messing with my head.
What can I do?
It's only a dream,
they say it's not real,
but here in my bed,
that's not how I feel.

WHO MADE THIS BOOK?
LET'S FIND OUT...

ABOUT THE POET

Edward van de Vendel was born in Leerdam, the Netherlands, in 1964. He taught in primary schools before becoming a full-time writer in 2001. He writes novels for children and young adults, poetry, picture books, non-fiction and song lyrics, which are published by Querido (Holland) and De Eenhoorn (Belgium).

His books have received many awards: Golden Kiss (Gouden Zoen/Gouden Lijst, best book for teenagers, four times), Silver Slate (Zilveren Griffel, best books for children, nine times), Woutertje Pieterse Prijs (critic's choice, twice), Children's Prize (Flanders, Belgium), the Prix Sorcières (France, best picture book) and the Deutsche Jugendliteraturpreis (Germany, best picture book).

He has four nominations for the Astrid Lindgren Memorial Award (2011/2012/2019/2020), and one for the Hans Christian Andersen Award (2018).

Photo: Jota Chabel

ABOUT THE TRANSLATOR

David Colmer is an Australian translator, writer and editor who lives in Amsterdam. He translates Dutch-language literature across a range of genres and has won several international prizes for his work.

His previous translations include four other books by Edward van de Vendel, among them two books of poetry: *I'll Root for You* and *The Sexy Storm*. Other recent translations include the modern Dutch classic *An Untouched House* by Willem Frederik Hermans and a collection of Jip and Janneke stories by the great Dutch children's author Annie M.G. Schmidt.

Photo: Michele Hutchison

ABOUT THE ILLUSTRATOR

Fleur van der Weel was born in 1970 in Middelburg, the Netherlands. When she was eighteen, Fleur moved to Amsterdam to study Law, which she didn't enjoy at all. Just before an important exam, she rang home in a panic and ended up following her mother's advice: 'My dear child, throw those law books in the canal and do something you like!' So she left the university and went to the Utrecht School of Arts instead.

Fleur is now an award-winning illustrator and has illustrated many children's books. She also makes animations for television. Fleur is always searching for simplicity in her drawings and she tries to tell an extra story alongside the text.

Super Guppy is the first book Fleur ever illustrated and it was a huge success, winning the Woutertje Pieterse Prize in 2004.

Photo: T. J. le Clercq

LEARN SOME DUTCH

The poems in this book were written in Dutch, which is the main official language of the Netherlands. We've picked out some words from the original Dutch poems and included a guide for how to say them (in brackets). Try to roll your *rrr*s, and pronounce 'g' and 'ch' like you do the 'ch' in Scottish loch (*ch*). Give it a go!

fish .... vis (fis)

cat .... poes (puss)

snow .... sneeuw (SNAY-oo)

blackbird .... merel (MEH-rull)

sea .... zee (zay)

spit .... spuug (spooo*ch*)

eyebrows .... wenkbrauwen (WENK-brow-en)

frog .... kikker (kickerrr)

fly away .... wegvliegen (WE*CH*-flee*ch*-en)

fruit .... fruit (frowt)

grandma .... oma (OH-ma)

you are sweet .... jij bent lief (yi bent leef)

shadow .... schaduw (S*CH*AH-doo)

dream .... droom (drome)

63

WRITE YOUR OWN POEMS

Now it's time to write your own poems and illustrate them too! Here are some ideas to help get you started.

We throw parties for all kinds of occasions: birthdays, weddings, moving into a new house, getting a new job. In 'Party' on page 4 they even throw a *catch up birthday* party. What's your favourite kind of party? **Write a poem about the best party you can imagine.** Think about all the details: who are the guests? What kind of food is there? Will there be games? What kind of decorations are there – balloons? Streamers? What will you wear? Is it fancy dress?

Do you have a pet? Or do you wish you did? In 'Fish' on page 5, we have no idea what the pet fish is trying to say. **Write poem about having a conversation with a real or imaginary pet.** What would you ask it? What might it reply?

 There's a decision to be made in 'Snow' on page 11: *'Run back inside where it's nice and warm or stay out and start a snowball fight?'* What would you rather do? **Write a poem about a snow day.** Start from the minute you know it's been snowing: does someone tell you or do you realise it by yourself? Then describe what you do next, bringing in as many senses as possible: what do you see? Smell? Hear? Feel? Taste?

In 'Wardrobe' on page 23 we learn about a good place to hide: *'Dad's wardrobe is my cubbyhole – I burrow in there like a mole'*. Do you have a favourite hiding place? What secret things do you get up to in there? Can others join you, or is it too small for visitors? **Write a poem about where you like to hide**, with every line starting 'Shhhh...' For example:

Shhhh... I'm under the stairs, behind the boxes of videotapes
Shhhh... I've come here to read my book in peace
Shhhh... I've brought a yoghurt and a spoon of jam

In 'Garden' on page 24 the garden gets a makeover. Do you have a garden? Or a favourite park? Does it have grass and hedges and flowers? A pond? A climbing frame? **Write a poem about your garden or favourite outside place.** What do you like about it?

In 'Window' on page 51, a bird is trying to get in through the window. Has an animal (that isn't a pet!) ever got into your house? What happened next? **Write a poem where an uninvited animal comes to stay...** What havoc do they cause?

• • •

We'd love to see what you come up with in response to these prompts! If you'd like us to take a look, email your poems and pictures to hello@theemmapress.com with 'Super Guppy poems' in the subject line.

ABOUT THE
EMMA PRESS

The Emma Press is a publishing house based in Birmingham, UK, run by Emma Dai'an Wright. It makes books for adults and children, specialising in poetry.

Emma Press books are starting to win prizes, including the Poetry Book Society Pamphlet Choice Award and the Saboteur Award for Best Collaborative Work. The Emma Press has been shortlisted for the Michael Marks Award for Poetry Pamphlet Publishers in 2014, 2015, 2016 and 2018, and actually won it in 2016 (hurray!).

Falling Out of the Sky: Poems about Myths and Monsters, the first Emma Press poetry book for children, was shortlisted for the 2016 CLiPPA, run by the Centre for Literacy in Primary Education. *Moon Juice*, a collection of poems by Kate Wakeling with illustrations by Elīna Braslina, won the CLiPPA in 2017.

You can find out more about The Emma Press and buy books directly from us here:

theemmapress.com